WHAT ARE MY OPTIONS?

What are my Options?

AN INTRODUCTION TO OPTIONS TRADING AND INVESTING

Carlos Ariel Then

Tyler Loiselle

Mr Then Consulting LLC

Contents

Disclaimer — vii
Foreword — ix

I
Understanding your Options — 1

1
What are Options? — 3

2
How do I Use Options? — 13

3
How can I get Options? — 21

II
Utilizing your Options — 27

4
Different Options — 28

5
Protecting your Options — 33

III
Controlling your Options 37

Last Option 41
Key Options Trading Terms and Explanations 43

Disclaimer

This publication, "What Are My Options?" (the "Book"), available in both physical and digital formats, is intended solely for informational purposes and does not constitute legal, financial, or other professional advice. The content within this Book should not be considered a replacement for professional consultation, diagnosis, or treatment.

The views expressed are those of the author and are presented "as is." No guarantees, either expressed or implied, are made regarding the completeness, accuracy, or reliability of the information in this Book. The author expressly disclaims all warranties, including but not limited to implied warranties of merchantability or fitness for a particular purpose. The author will not be liable for any losses, injuries, or damages resulting from the interpretation or use of the Book.

Reproduction, storage in a retrieval system, or transmission in any form or by any means—electronic, mechanical, photocopying, recording, or otherwise—without prior written permission from the author is strictly prohibited.

This Book is not intended as a definitive guide for any specific situation. Readers should always seek professional advice from qualified individuals regarding their unique circumstances. Neither the author nor any parties involved in the creation, production, or distribution of this Book shall be liable for any direct, indirect, consequential, incidental, special, or punitive damages arising from its use.

The author reserves the right to alter the contents of this Book at any time without notice and does not assume any responsibility for errors, inaccuracies, or omissions found within.

By accessing, downloading, or using this Book, you are agreeing to the terms and conditions stated herein. If you do not agree with these terms, you should not access, download, or use this Book.

Foreword

At some point in everyone's life, they come to the realization that options become opportunities. And if you look back on your life you see all the real options you have had so far, even though you may not have seen them at the time. Luckily, you have so many in front of you.

When our paths first crossed, I don't think Carlos and I even came close to understanding the opportunities that would lie ahead of us. Each of us still in school, each on the path of becoming what we truly wanted in life and each of us knocking on every door that would get us there. It is a credit to our families, our educators and our life teachers, whether it was the coaches, mentors or friends along the way. They hammered the idea that we have no limits and so many options.

Our paths were so different, but also so alike. I knew Carlos was ready for the world early on and knew he would bring a lot to the table. All of the services he offers, his countless educational tools for people who want to learn and his friendship makes him an invaluable resource.

His entrepreneurial spirit was spotted early, not just by myself, but by a number of our fellow employees and supervisors. He handled every customer interaction not as if they were a customer of the corporation, but as if they were a close and personal friend seeking a service from his own company. And here we are, more than 13 years later and he personally services friends, family and clients with credit help, investment help and nearly any other financial need a person could have.

Carlos' wisdom didn't come with age, it came with experience. He took on a lot of work early on, and still rarely, if ever, says no. He accepts every challenge and faces it head on. And because of this, our vision for the future as individuals aligned. Who doesn't want financial freedom? Who doesn't want to take advantage of investing with a measured risk/reward?

Carlos first introduced me to option contracts a few years ago. It took me a bit to dive in, but his explanation made it worth checking out. I asked countless questions and he almost always knew the answer and would share the knowledge. If he didn't we would have learned the answer together.

The stock market can be intimidating. There is so much information out there and endless amounts of research you can do, and that research is completely justifiable. Market conditions change daily and information comes constantly and that makes it even more overwhelming. Which is why a book like this is needed. It is a reliable and practical resource that you will be able to dive into when you need a refresher.

Like anything, you have to be willing to learn. Approach each learning with an open mind, and never be afraid to learn by doing. The lessons in investing can be applied to so many real world and life situations. You've already started by investing in yourself by investing in this book.

This book will teach you how to use options in the stock market to help leverage your investment portfolio and give you the knowledge to utilize options, but even beyond that it will show you ways to apply opportunity to your life.

When people say the often overused "someone has so much untapped potential" they are typically referring to someone not taking advantage of every option they've been given and the options still to come, hoping the person makes the "right" decision for them. I hope you have this book in your hands at an opportune time to take advantage of your own opportunities that lie ahead.

I

Understanding your Options

At the crossroads of financial wilderness

Picture this: You're standing at a crossroads in the financial wilderness, where every path is shrouded in mystery and potential. You've heard the whispers of options trading, an elusive yet intriguing world where fortunes are made and lost in the blink of an eye. It's a world that demands more than just guts - it demands savvy, strategy, and an appetite for risk.

Let's cut through the fog. You've played the stock market game - straightforward, almost routine - buy low, sell high. But here's the twist: navigating the labyrinth of options trading is a whole different ball game. It's not just about the money in your account; it's about the decisions you make with it.

I remember staring at my own trading screen, the numbers flashing like a casino jackpot, wondering if I had what it takes to dive into the deep end of options. It's a world where Strike Prices, Expiration Dates, and those Greek alphabets that dictate market behaviors aren't just terms; they're your tools for sculpting success or courting disaster.

Did I dare to venture? You bet I did. And let me tell you, it wasn't a blind leap but a calculated stride into a realm where control isn't just a word, but your most valuable asset. Options trading opened a door to a dimension where risk could be tailored and rewards magnified.

As you turn these pages, you might feel a surge of skepticism. "Too complex," you might think, or "Maybe I'll stick to what I know." But isn't life about exploration, about pushing boundaries? This isn't just another trading guide; it's a map to a treasure trove for the brave.

So, what's it going to be? Will you take the familiar path, or will you step into the world of options, where the potential is as vast as the risks? Your journey into the heart of financial alchemy begins now. Let's find out if options trading is your undiscovered country.

1

What are Options?

Welcome to the captivating world of options trading, a realm where each decision weaves the fabric of potential financial futures. To navigate this complex terrain, let's draw an analogy to something more tangible and familiar – real estate wholesaling. Understanding this concept provides a lucid lens through which we can view the intricate nature of options trading.

Real Estate Wholesaling: A Prelude to Options

Real estate wholesaling is akin to being a strategic middleman in the property market. As a wholesaler, you identify a property—often undervalued or in need of attention—and secure a contract to buy it. But here's the twist: instead of completing the purchase, you assign this contract to an investor or buyer, profiting from the price differential. This process is a dance of negotiation, understanding market value, and foreseeing potential, much like options trading.

Options Trading: The Financial Equivalent of Wholesaling

In the financial markets, options trading plays a similar role. Here, options are akin to contracts that grant you the right—but not the obligation—to buy or sell an asset, like stocks, at a pre-determined 'strike price.' It's like having a reserved opportunity to buy a property at a specific price, with the freedom to follow through or assign this chance to someone else.

The Power of Contracts

Both real estate wholesaling and options trading derive their power from the contract. In wholesaling, your contract offers control over a property transaction without the need for outright ownership. In options trading, the contract gives you control over stock movements without needing to own the stock itself.

Leveraging Opportunities

Leverage plays a pivotal role in both domains. In wholesaling, a small earnest deposit can hold the key to a potentially lucrative property deal. Similarly, in options trading, a relatively modest investment can control a significant portion of stock, setting the stage for potentially significant returns.

Navigating Risks and Rewards

Effective risk management is crucial in both fields. Just as a real estate wholesaler needs to understand property trends and buyer interests, an options trader must grasp market dynamics and investor psychology. Both demand an astute sense of speculation, calculated risks, and an eye for opportunity.

The Thrill of Speculation

At their core, both wholesaling and options trading are grounded in the art of speculation. Wholesalers bet on property values and market demand; options traders place their stakes on stock price movements and market shifts.

As we journey through this book, our goal is to demystify options trading, making it as accessible and understandable as real estate wholesaling. We aim to equip you with the knowledge to confidently make choices, whether on Wall Street's tumultuous trading floors or in the vibrant real estate market of Main Street. Let's embark on this exploration into the world of options trading, where every decision is a gateway to new financial opportunities and a testament to the power of strategic choice.

Is Options Trading the Right Path for You?

As we navigate the intricate world of options trading, it's crucial to pause and consider: is this journey right for you? While the allure of mastering options trading is strong, it's not a path suited for everyone. The financial market, often seen as a battlefield where the impatient inadvertently enrich the patient, demands more than just a desire to participate—it requires readiness and aptitude. Here are six signs that options trading might not align with your financial journey:

Unclear on Options Trading Basics: If the concept of options trading is still a puzzle to you, even with experience in other trading forms like Forex, Crypto, or Stocks, tread cautiously. Options trading involves unique risks and strategies. Without a solid foundation in these basics, venturing into options might be premature.

Risk Aversion: Central to options trading is the acceptance of risk. If the thought of potential financial loss unsettles you deeply, this might not be your arena. Options trading requires a stomach for risk and an ability to manage it effectively.

Limited Financial Market Understanding: The broader financial markets are complex ecosystems. A comprehensive understanding is essential for making informed trading decisions. Without this, diving into options trading could be like setting sail without a map.

Impatience: Patience isn't just a virtue in options trading; it's a necessity. The market demands a calm, collected approach, waiting for the right moment to strike. If impulsive decisions are more your style, options trading may prove challenging.

Seeking a Gambling Alternative: If you're transitioning from gambling, seeking a similar thrill in the financial markets, options trading might not be the solution. While it can offer excitement, the stakes and potential for loss are considerably higher, often exceeding the gambling tables.

The Illusion of Quick, Easy Money: If you're under the impression that options trading is a shortcut to wealth, reconsider. This field requires diligent study, strategic planning, and often, a long-term commitment to see substantial returns.

Understanding these cautionary points helps in evaluating whether options trading aligns with your financial goals and temperament. It's about knowing yourself, your tolerance for risk, and your willingness to learn. If these warnings resonate with you, it might be wise to explore other avenues in the financial landscape where your skills and temperament find a better fit.

Having explored the foundational aspects of options trading, let's delve further into its core components – specifically, 'calls' and 'puts', which are the building blocks of options strategies.

Understanding Calls and Puts

Call Options

- Imagine you're eyeing a potential investment property. You believe its value will rise, but you're not ready to commit to buying it yet. A call option is akin to paying a small fee to reserve the right to buy that property at today's price, within a set time frame. In the stock market, buying a call option means you're paying for the right to purchase a particular stock at a specified price (the strike price) before the option expires. If the stock's price rises above your strike price, your call option becomes more valuable as you have the right to buy the stock cheaper than the current market price.

Put Options

- Conversely, let's say you own a property but are concerned about a potential drop in the market. A put option is like having an agreement to sell your property at a current favorable price, regardless of future market dips. In trading, buying a put option gives you the right to sell a specific stock at a predetermined price before the option expires. If the stock's price falls below your strike price, the put option increases in value since you can sell the stock at a higher price than the current market value.

Other Key Concepts in Options Trading

- **Strike Price:** This is the set price at which an option can be exercised. It's like the agreed-upon price for buying or selling the property in our real estate analogy.
- **Expiration Date:** Options don't last forever. They have an expiration date, which is the final day the option can be exercised. It's similar to the closing date in a real estate contract.
- **Premium:** This is the cost of buying an option. It's like a non-refundable deposit you pay for the right to buy or sell an asset at the strike price.
- **Intrinsic and Extrinsic Value:** The intrinsic value is how much the option is worth if exercised right now. The extrinsic value, on the other hand, includes factors like time remaining until expiration and stock volatility.
- **The Greeks:** These are measures that help traders assess various risks associated with options. The most commonly known are Delta (measuring the rate of change in the option price), Theta (time decay of the option), and Vega (sensitivity to volatility).

As we continue through this book, we'll explore each of these components in detail, providing you with a comprehensive understanding of how options work. We'll also discuss various strategies that can be employed using calls and puts, helping you to navigate the options market with greater confidence.

Remember, options trading is not just about understanding the terminology; it's about seeing the potential in each option, much like a visionary sees potential in a piece of land. It's a journey of learning, analyzing, and making strategic decisions that align with your investment goals. Let's embark on this journey together, unlocking the secrets of options trading one step at a time.

As we delve deeper into the world of options trading, let's simplify some key concepts using everyday analogies. Think of call and put options in terms of a phone call - when you 'pick up' a call, the conversation (or the stock price) is going up; when you 'put down' the phone, it signifies the end or a downward movement. This analogy can help demystify these fundamental elements of options trading.

A call option in the stock market is like picking up a phone to answer a call. When you buy a call option, you're anticipating that the stock's price will rise - much like 'picking up' on an opportunity. You're paying for the right (but not the obligation) to buy a stock at a specific price within a certain timeframe. If the stock price climbs above your strike price (the price you agreed to pay), your call option increases in value, mirroring the action of 'picking up' a profitable call.

Conversely, a put option is akin to putting down the phone. This option is used when you expect a stock's price to fall. By purchasing a put option, you secure the right to sell a stock at a predetermined price. If the market price drops below your strike price, the put option's value goes up. It's like 'putting down' a protective barrier against declining stock values, ensuring you can still sell at a higher price.

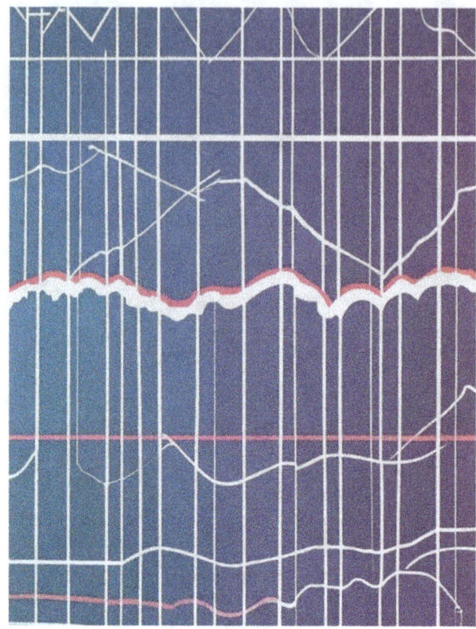

Beyond calls and puts, understanding trend lines is crucial in options trading. Trend lines are like the storyline of a phone conversation; they show the direction in which a stock price is moving. By drawing trend lines on stock charts, you can identify patterns and predict future movements. These lines can show an upward trend (an ascending line), a downward trend (a descending line), or a sideways movement (a flat line). Understanding these trends helps you decide when to 'pick up' a call option or 'put down' a put option.

As we move forward in this book, we'll explore how to use calls and puts effectively, and how trend lines can guide your trading decisions. We'll look at real-life examples to illustrate these concepts, making options trading less about complex financial jargon and more about intuitive, informed decision-making. Think of this journey as learning a new language, where each term and strategy helps you better converse with the world of finance. Let's continue to uncover the opportunities and protections that options trading offers, turning these concepts into practical tools for your investment goals.

Foundations of Options Trading

As we continue to unravel the essence of options trading, it's crucial to establish a strong foundational understanding. We've covered the basics of calls and puts and the analogy of a phone conversation to simplify these concepts. Now, let's enrich this foundation with more crucial elements necessary for anyone starting in options trading.

Options: American vs. European

Options come in different flavors. The most common types are American and European options. The key difference lies in when you can exercise them. American options allow you to exercise the option at any time before expiration, providing more flexibility. European options, however, can only be exercised on the expiration date itself. This distinction is vital in strategy planning.

Options Trading: The Importance of Volatility

Volatility is a critical concept in the options world. It refers to how much the price of an asset, such as a stock, fluctuates. High volatility means the stock price can change dramatically in a short period, while low volatility indicates less dramatic movements. Options traders need to understand volatility because it significantly impacts the value of an option. High volatility often means higher option premiums, as the potential for profit - and risk - increases.

The Role of Time Decay

In options trading, time is a double-edged sword, known as 'time decay.' The value of options decreases as the expiration date approaches, especially if the stock price is far from the strike price. This concept is crucial for options sellers, as time decay can work in their favor, and for buyers to understand the urgency of market movements in relation to their options.

Understanding Liquidity in Options Trading

Liquidity refers to how easily you can buy or sell an asset without affecting its price. In options trading, liquidity is vital because it impacts your ability to execute trades quickly and at predictable prices. Options on highly liquid stocks will generally have tighter bid-ask spreads, meaning the difference between the buying and selling price is smaller, which is advantageous for traders.

Risk Management: Essential for Options Traders

A cornerstone of successful options trading is effective risk management. This involves understanding the maximum potential loss and gain for every trade, using stop-loss orders to limit losses, and diversifying your options portfolio. Risk management ensures that you stay in the game, even when some trades don't go as planned.

Getting Started with a Broker

To start trading options, you need a brokerage account. It's essential to choose a broker that offers a trading platform which suits your needs, with reasonable fees, and educational resources for options traders. Many brokers also offer paper trading - a way to practice options trading without risking real money, which is highly recommended for beginners.

As we conclude this chapter, remember that options trading is not just about understanding terms and concepts. It's about developing a strategic mindset, being aware of the risks involved, and continuously learning and adapting to the market's rhythms. With this solid foundation, you're now ready to delve into the deeper strategies and nuances of options trading in the coming chapters. Let's embark on this journey with both caution and excitement, as we explore the vast potential that options trading has to offer.

How do I Use Options?

Stepping into the second chapter of our journey into options trading, we delve into the practical application of options. Personally, I've found a blend of protection and speculation to be an effective approach. This dual strategy is exemplified by the "Collar" or "Protective Put" method.

The Protective Put Strategy

The Protective Put is a savvy approach where you buy a put option and simultaneously sell a call option. Here's how it works:

- The put option grants you the right (but not the obligation) to sell the underlying asset at a pre-set price, known as the strike price. This is your safety net, protecting your portfolio against potential losses if the asset's price drops below this threshold. It's important to remember that no strategy is entirely risk-free.
- The call option, meanwhile, gives you the right to buy the same asset at the strike price. This plays into the speculative aspect of the strategy, where you can profit if the asset's price rises above the strike price and your put option expires without value.

Developing Your Options Trading Approach

Now, to tailor options trading to your specific goals, follow these steps:

- Choose Your Strategy: Start by deciding on your strategy. Will you adopt the Protective Put, or do you have another approach in mind? Commit to your chosen strategy.
- Select the Underlying Asset: Decide what you want to trade – stocks, commodities, indices? Focus on an asset class or even a specific stock and stick with it.
- Identify the Right Option: Determine whether you need a put or a call option, the strike price, and the expiration date. Analyze the options chain to compare prices and find the option that aligns with your strategy.
- Place Your Order: Once you've identified the right option, place your order through your broker.
- Monitor the Market: Stay vigilant and monitor market movements. If the market trends in your favor, you may opt to stay the course. If it moves against you, consider exiting the trade to cut losses.

Sticking to the Plan

One of the critical pitfalls in options trading is failing to adhere to your plan. Shifting strategies, changing the underlying asset, or constantly switching options types can lead to losses. Diversification is different from switching; it involves varying your investments while staying true to your fundamental strategy. Avoid making impulsive changes – consistency is key.

Managing Costs and Risks

To manage the costs associated with premiums, maintain a positive risk-to-reward ratio. Aim for larger gains on winning trades compared to losses on the unsuccessful ones. Utilizing stop-loss orders can help automate this process, closing trades at a predetermined price to prevent further losses.

In this chapter, we'll explore these aspects in greater detail, providing you with the tools and knowledge to effectively use options in your trading repertoire. We'll look at different strategies, how to execute them, and ways to manage risks and costs. By the end of this chapter, you'll have a clearer understanding of how to use options not just as financial instruments, but as powerful tools in your investment strategy. Let's dive in and unlock the full potential of options trading.

Navigating the Use of Options

Having established a fundamental understanding of options and an overview of strategy selection, let's delve deeper into the practical aspects of using options effectively, setting the stage for more complex strategies we'll explore in Chapter Four.

Understanding Option Pricing

To use options effectively, comprehending how they are priced is crucial. Option pricing is influenced by several factors:

- Underlying Asset's Price: The current price of the stock or asset linked to the option directly impacts the option's price.
- Strike Price: The closer the strike price is to the current market price, the more valuable the option typically is.
- Expiration Date: Generally, the more time until the option expires, the higher the premium, as it allows more time for the asset to move favorably.
- Volatility: Higher volatility in the asset's price can increase the option's price since there is a greater chance of the option ending up in-the-money.

- Interest Rates and Dividends: These can also affect option pricing, though their impact is usually less pronounced than the other factors.

Basic Order Types in Options Trading

When placing options trades, familiarize yourself with different order types:

- Market Orders: Buy or sell an option immediately at the current market price.
- Limit Orders: Set a specific price at which you want to buy or sell an option. The trade only executes if the market price reaches your set limit.
- Stop Orders: These are designed to limit losses or protect profits. A stop order turns into a market order once the stock reaches a certain price.

Managing Risks in Options Trading

Understanding and managing risks are paramount in options trading:

- Capital Allocation: Never invest more than you can afford to lose. A common rule of thumb is not to allocate more than 5-10% of your portfolio to any single options trade.
- Diversification: Spread your risk across different assets and types of options trades.
- Understanding Leverage: Options can provide significant leverage, which can amplify both gains and losses. Be mindful of the leverage each options contract represents and manage it wisely.

Research and Analysis

Before entering any options trade, thorough research and analysis are essential:

- Fundamental Analysis: Evaluate the underlying asset's financial health, including earnings, market position, and future prospects.
- Technical Analysis: Use chart patterns and indicators to predict future price movements and identify potential trading opportunities.

Monitoring and Adjusting Your Positions

Options trading requires active management:

- Regularly monitor your open positions and the overall market conditions.
- Be prepared to adjust or close your positions based on changing market dynamics or as your options approach expiration.

Record Keeping and Review

Maintaining detailed records of your trades is crucial for learning and improvement:

- Keep track of your trades, including the rationale behind each decision.
- Regularly review your trades to assess your performance and learn from both successes and mistakes.

As we further explore the essentials of options trading, it's important to deepen our understanding of key concepts and practices. This knowledge forms the bedrock upon which successful trading strategies are built.

The Importance of Timing in Options Trading

Timing is a critical factor in options trading. Understanding market cycles and the best times to enter or exit a trade can significantly impact your success. This includes being aware of earnings announcements, economic reports, and other events that can affect stock prices.

Leveraging Technical Indicators

Technical indicators are tools that can help predict future market trends and price movements. Some common indicators used in options trading include:

- Moving Averages: Indicate the average stock price over a specific period, helping identify trends.
- Relative Strength Index (RSI): Measures the magnitude of recent price changes to evaluate overbought or oversold conditions.
- Bollinger Bands: Consist of a set of trendlines plotted two standard deviations away from a simple moving average, indicating volatility.

Developing a Trading Plan

Every successful trader needs a solid trading plan. This should include:

- Investment Goals: Clearly define your short-term and long-term financial objectives.
- Risk Tolerance: Understand how much risk you are willing to take.
- Entry and Exit Strategies: Determine when to enter a trade and, more importantly, when to exit, whether in profit or loss.

Staying Informed

Staying updated with market news and trends is vital. This can include:

- Financial News: Regularly follow financial news through trusted sources to stay informed about market-moving events.
- Economic Calendars: Keep an eye on economic calendars for important events that could impact the markets.

Continuous Learning and Adaptation

The world of options trading is ever-evolving. Continuous learning is key to staying ahead:

- Educational Resources: Utilize books, courses, webinars, and seminars to enhance your knowledge.
- Networking with Other Traders: Engage with a community of traders to share insights and learn from their experiences.

Practicing with Paper Trading

Before risking real capital, consider practicing with paper trading (simulated trading). This allows you to test strategies and get a feel for the market without financial risk.

Balancing Emotions

Trading can be an emotional rollercoaster. Maintaining emotional balance is crucial:

- Avoid Emotional Trading: Decisions should be based on logic and analysis, not emotions like fear or greed.
- Stress Management: Develop techniques to manage stress effectively, ensuring it doesn't impact your trading decisions.

In summary, mastering options trading requires a blend of knowledge, strategic planning, and emotional control. As we move forward in this chapter, we will consolidate these elements, empowering you with a comprehensive toolkit to navigate the options market. With this foundation, you will be well-prepared to tackle more advanced strategies and make informed decisions in your trading journey.

3

____

How can I get Options?

Welcome to Chapter Three, where we dive into the crucial process of seeking and selecting the right options for your trading strategy. It's not just about finding a good broker or a promising asset; it's about a meticulous and informed approach to identifying the best opportunities for options trading.

Understanding the Hunt for Options

Seeking options is an art, requiring a keen eye for detail and a strategic mindset. It's not just about jumping into any opportunity but about being discerning and selecting the ones that align with your goals and strategies.

Analyzing the Underlying Asset

The first step is a thorough analysis of the underlying asset. This involves understanding the asset's performance, market trends, and potential future movements. The public's perception, indicated by the open interest, is a valuable gauge of the asset's popularity.

Interpreting Open Interest

Open interest represents the total number of outstanding contracts (options and futures). High open interest typically signifies a popular underlying asset, suggesting a more liquid and potentially more attractive options market for that asset.

Gauging Volatility

Volatility measures the degree of price movement in the underlying asset. High volatility often indicates a greater likelihood of price movements aligning with your anticipated direction. While high volatility can present greater opportunities, it also comes with increased risk.

The Four Filters for Option Selection

To refine your search for the right options, apply these four filters:

1. Volatility Health: Avoid unhealthy volatility periods, like those around holidays or events that could disrupt normal market conditions.
2. Open Interest Health: Look for assets with healthy open interest, indicating a robust and liquid market.
3. Time-per-Trade: Consider the duration you intend to hold the option. The longer the time, the more patience required for the trade to unfold.
4. Market Sentiment: Assess the overall market sentiment towards the underlying asset. Are investors bullish (expecting prices to rise) or bearish (expecting prices to fall)?

Setting Clear Goals

Before diving into options trading, it's imperative to have clear goals. What do you seek to achieve through options trading? Your objectives will guide your strategy, choice of assets, and types of options to pursue. Without a clear understanding of your goals, it's easy to get lost in the myriad of choices and market noise.

The Importance of Caution and Knowledge

Options trading is not an arena for impulsive decisions or un-informed risks. If you're unsure about a particular trade or strategy, it's better to step back and seek more information or consult with more experienced traders. Remember, in the world of options, knowledge is power, and caution is a valuable ally.

As we progress through this chapter, we will delve into practical methods and tools to help you identify and select the right options, aligning with your trading goals and risk tolerance. This chapter is designed to empower you with the skills to sift through the options market, picking out the gems that fit your investment strategy. Let's embark on this journey of discovery, learning to discern the right options that will pave your path to trading success.

What if no option is in sight?

Finding and Capitalizing on Options Opportunities

In this chapter, we continue our exploration into how one can actively seek and capitalize on options trading opportunities, even when they aren't immediately apparent.

When Options Seem Scarce

If you find yourself in a situation where no viable option seems in sight, don't be discouraged. This doesn't signify a dead end, but rather a call to refine your search. Successful trading often involves as much research and preparation as it does actual trading. If you're struggling to find suitable options, revisit the four filters we discussed earlier. Here's how to enhance your search:

- News Events as Catalysts: Stay updated with news events, but don't rely on them for impulsive trades. Trading on news requires a strategy. Wait for price action confirmation following an announcement before making your move. For instance, if a key economic report like the Consumer Price Index (CPI) is released, observe the market's reaction and look for a confirmed trading signal rather than jumping in immediately.

- Pattern Analysis: Candlestick and chart patterns are invaluable tools for traders. They can provide insights into market sentiment and potential price movements. Look for patterns that indicate reversals or continuations in trends, as these can signal entry points for options trades.
- Volume Monitoring: Volume analysis can reveal the strength or weakness of a trend. An increasing volume can indicate a strong trend, which might be a good time to enter a trade. Conversely, decreasing volume might suggest it's better to steer clear.
- Using Technical Indicators: Indicators like moving averages, RSI, stochastic oscillators, and MACD can offer objective entry signals for options trading. Each of these indicators serves a specific purpose:
  - Moving Averages: Useful for identifying trends. Watch for short-term averages crossing over long-term ones for potential entry signals.
  - Relative Strength Index (RSI): Helps identify overbought or oversold conditions. An RSI above 70 suggests overbought conditions, while below 30 indicates oversold.
  - Stochastic Oscillator: Excellent for spotting divergences and potential market reversals, especially useful in ranging markets.
  - MACD: Ideal for identifying early trend changes through moving average crossovers.

Understanding the Time Element in Options

Unlike other financial instruments, options trading involves a time component. When you buy an option, you're not only speculating on the asset's price movement but also on the time frame in which it will occur. This adds a layer of complexity to your trading decisions and should be a key consideration in your strategy.

Establishing a Routine

Regularly scanning the markets, staying informed about global events, and continuously analyzing charts and data should be part of your daily routine as an options trader. This consistent approach will help you identify opportunities more effectively and make well-informed decisions.

Refining Your Approach to Options Trading

As we conclude this chapter, let's solidify your approach to seeking and selecting the right options, ensuring you are well-equipped to navigate the markets confidently and effectively.

Establishing a Consistent Research Methodology

Consistency in your research approach is key. Develop a routine that involves reviewing financial news, analyzing market trends, and studying historical data. This consistent approach will enhance your ability to spot viable options trading opportunities.

Adapting to Market Changes

The financial markets are dynamic and ever-changing. Flexibility and adaptability are crucial in options trading. Be prepared to adjust your strategies in response to market shifts. Continuous learning and staying attuned to global economic developments will help you pivot as needed.

Utilizing Technology and Tools

Leverage technology to your advantage. Utilize trading platforms and tools that offer advanced charting capabilities, real-time data, and analytical features. Many platforms also provide options-specific tools, such as probability calculators and options scanners, which can aid in your decision-making process.

Building a Support Network

Engage with a community of traders and participate in forums or groups where you can exchange ideas and strategies. Learning from the experiences of others can provide valuable insights and enhance your trading skills.

Practicing Risk Management

Always prioritize risk management in your trading. This involves setting stop-loss orders, diversifying your options portfolio, and only investing capital that you can afford to lose. Remember, effective risk management is the cornerstone of sustainable trading.

Keeping Emotions in Check

Options trading can be exhilarating but also stressful. Managing your emotions is critical. Develop a mindset that allows you to make rational decisions based on data and analysis, rather than impulsive reactions to market fluctuations.

Setting Realistic Expectations

Lastly, set realistic expectations. Options trading can be profitable, but it's not a guaranteed path to quick riches. Approach trading with a mindset of gradual growth and learning. Celebrate your successes, learn from your losses, and continually strive to improve your skills.

As we wrap up this chapter, remember that finding and capitalizing on options trading opportunities requires a blend of research, strategy, risk management, and emotional control. With the foundations laid in this chapter, you're now better prepared to venture into the more advanced aspects of options trading, where we will explore specific strategies and techniques to enhance your trading journey. Let's move forward with the knowledge and skills to make informed, strategic decisions in the vibrant world of options trading.

II

Utilizing your Options

I, personally, am not a big fan of gambling, but I do appreciate the opportunity to take a calculated risk. Options trading, similar to a calculated gamble, presents an opportunity to manage risk while aiming for potential gains. It's a challenging yet rewarding arena, demanding a deep understanding of various strategies and market behaviors. This chapter delves into different options strategies, equipping you with the tools to tailor your approach to varying market conditions.

Options trading can be extremely profitable if done correctly. With the right amount of research and practice, you can make money by understanding the complexities of this type of trading.

It's important to understand that while you can make money trading options, you can also lose as much money as you can make. Success in options trading not only asks for a lot of research and practice but also a keen understanding of the market and its movements.

To utilize your options means understanding the basics of options trading and the different strategies that are available. When you have a better understanding of these strategies, you can begin to make better decisions with your trades.

4

Different Options

Options strategies serve as tools in a trader's toolbox, each with its own set of advantages and disadvantages. No single strategy is universally applicable, as their effectiveness depends on market conditions. For instance, during volatile periods, traders may opt for strategies that capitalize on market direction, whereas in uptrends, they may choose methods that benefit from a steady market. A trader's ability to employ various strategies enhances their potential for profitability in diverse market conditions.

Here are the different options trading strategies:

1. **Credit Spreads**: These involve simultaneous buying and selling of options, resulting in a net credit. This strategy relies on probability rather than substantial gains and requires careful selection based on market conditions.
2. **Bull Call Spread**: It involves buying a call option at a lower strike price and selling another call at a higher strike price, suitable for moderate upward price expectations.
3. **Bear Put Spread**: This strategy involves buying a put option at a higher strike price and selling another put at a lower strike

price, used when expecting a moderate decline in the underlying asset.

4. **Box Spread**: An advanced strategy that combines bull call and bear put spreads, offering limited and defined gains and losses.

5. **Volatility Strategies**: These strategies capitalize on expected significant price movements, irrespective of their direction.

6. **Long Straddle**: Involves buying both a call and a put at the same strike price, profiting from substantial price movements in either direction.

7. **Short Straddle**: Requires selling both a call and a put at the same strike price, benefiting from minimal price movement.

8. **Long Strangle**: Involves buying out-of-the-money call and put options, requiring a lower initial investment compared to a straddle.

9. **Short Strangle**: Profitable in stagnant markets but carries unlimited risk if significant market movements occur.

10. **Directional Strategies**: These strategies use calls or puts to bet on the direction of a stock's price movement.

11. **Long Call/Put Options**: Used when anticipating upward or downward price movements, respectively.

12. **Covered Calls/Puts**: Involves owning the underlying asset and selling call or put options to generate income, providing some downside protection.

13. **Protective Collar**: Combines a protective put with a covered call to limit downside risk while allowing for some upside potential.

14. **Combination Strategies**: These strategies combine multiple positions to create unique risk/reward profiles.

15. **Butterfly Spread**: Combines bull and bear spreads with three different strike prices, offering a neutral risk/reward profile.

16. **Iron Condor**: Involves selling out-of-the-money call and put options while buying further out-of-the-money call and put options, benefiting from low volatility.

17. **Calendar Spread**: Profits from time decay by selling a short-term option and buying a longer-term option of the same type and strike price.

18. **Strangle/Strap**: Involves buying or selling out-of-the-money calls and puts, with potentially unlimited gains and risks.

19. **Hedging Strategies**: Used to protect existing positions from adverse price movements.

20. **Synthetic Positions**: Combine options and stock positions to mimic other trading strategies, used for hedging or modifying portfolio risk.

21. **Collars and Protective Puts**: Provide downside protection for stock holdings, limiting potential losses.

While exploring these strategies, keep in mind that each carries its own set of risks and rewards. Successful options trading relies on understanding these strategies, evaluating market conditions, and aligning trades with your financial goals and risk tolerance. Subsequent sections of this book will delve into each strategy in detail, offering insights and examples to enhance your trading skills.

As we venture further into advanced options strategies, let's break them down into more accessible terms, making them understandable even for those new to financial terminology.

- **Delta Neutral Trading Simplified**: Think of it as balancing on a seesaw, adjusting your position to remain balanced, regardless of small shifts. It's about reducing risk from price fluctuations by maintaining a balanced overall position.

- **Iron Butterflies Made Easy**: Similar to a safety net for a tightrope walker, it catches you if the market doesn't move much. You sell options at the current stock price and buy options slightly further out. If the stock price stays stable, you're safe; too much movement, and the net limits your gain or loss.

- **Diagonal Spreads Explained**: Picture a road trip with two cars—one for the entire journey and one swapped at various points. Diagonal spreads use options with different expiration times and prices to play with time and price, aiming to profit over a longer period.

- **Pair Trading with Options for Beginners**: Think of it like a three-legged race with two friends who must move together. You take two correlated stocks and use options to manage risk and potentially profit from their relative performance.

- **Synthetic Options Unpacked**: Imagine creating a recipe where you mix stock and options to mimic traditional options, often at a lower cost or with different risk characteristics.

- **Risk Reversal Strategy in Layman's Terms**: It's like betting on a horse race but betting on one horse to win and another not to lose. Risk reversal involves using options to express a bullish or bearish view on a stock without buying or selling the stock itself.

- **Strips and Straps Broken Down**: These are like adjusting a bet on a coin toss based on your expectation of heads or tails landing more often.

- **Rolling Options Forward Explained**: Think of it as renewing a lease on an apartment to extend your stay. Rolling options forward allows you to maintain or adjust your position without closing it entirely.

As we explore these strategies, remember that the goal is to manage risk and capitalize on market movements, aligning with your investment goals. Subsequent sections will provide in-depth insights on how to implement these strategies, when to use them, and how they fit into your overall trading plan. Options trading can be complex, but breaking down each strategy into understandable segments aims to make it more navigable and less intimidating for traders at all levels. Continue your journey into the nuanced world of options trading, empowered with knowledge to explore its potential with confidence.

Looking ahead, Chapter Five will focus on "Protecting Your Options." This crucial aspect of options trading is about safeguarding your investments and managing risks effectively. We'll delve into protective strategies that help you preserve capital and minimize losses, essential for long-term success in the volatile world of options trading.

Key Takeaways for Successful Options Trading

- Research and Continuous Learning: Stay informed about market trends, economic indicators, and news events that could impact your trading decisions.
- Risk Management: Always prioritize managing your risks. Utilize stop-loss orders, diversify your portfolio, and only invest capital you can afford to lose.
- Emotional Discipline: Maintain a disciplined approach to trading, keeping emotions like fear and greed in check.
- Record Keeping: Keep a detailed record of your trades to analyze your performance and learn from both successes and mistakes.

Setting the Stage for Chapter Five

In the next chapter, we will explore various protective measures and strategies, such as protective puts, stop-loss orders, and diversification techniques. These tools are vital in ensuring that your options trading journey is not only profitable but also sustainable over the long term.

As we conclude this chapter, take a moment to reflect on the strategies discussed and consider how they fit into your overall trading plan. Remember, the key to mastering options trading lies not just in understanding individual strategies, but in knowing when and how to apply them effectively.

5

Protecting your Options

In Chapter Five, we shift our focus from strategy execution to the vital aspect of options trading: protection. Protecting your options is about safeguarding your capital, managing risks, and maintaining emotional discipline. Let's delve into the various facets of protection in options trading.

Risk Management: The First Line of Defense

Risk management is the cornerstone of successful options trading. It encompasses various strategies and tools designed to minimize potential losses.

- Stop Loss Orders: A fundamental tool for risk management, stop-loss orders automatically close a position at a predetermined price level. It's essential to set these orders thoughtfully, balancing the need to protect against loss without triggering premature exits due to market noise.

- Hedging: Hedging strategies, like buying a put option while holding a call option, can help offset potential losses. This approach provides insurance against adverse market movements, effectively balancing your position.

- Diversification: Spreading your investments across different asset classes or sectors can reduce overall risk. Incorporating assets like commodities or currencies into your portfolio provides broader market exposure and can hedge against sector-specific risks.
- Long-Term Planning: Beyond immediate trades, consider your long-term financial goals. Adopting a long-term perspective can guide more balanced trading decisions, favoring sustainable growth over short-term gains.

Emotional Discipline: Keeping Your Cool

Emotional discipline is as critical as any technical strategy in options trading.

- Understanding Emotional Triggers: Recognize emotions like fear, greed, and impatience that can cloud judgment. Awareness is the first step to gaining control over these emotional responses.
- Sticking to the Plan: Discipline in adhering to your trading plan is key. This includes defined entry and exit points, risk per trade, and types of trades you're comfortable with.
- Practicing Patience: Avoid rash decisions. Allow yourself time to evaluate trades thoroughly. Patience is a vital trait in navigating the often turbulent waters of the options market.

Protecting Profits: Locking in Gains

While minimizing losses is important, so is protecting and realizing profits.

- Profit Targets: Establish clear profit targets for each trade. Once these targets are reached, consider taking profits to avoid potential market reversals.
- Trailing Stop Losses: Adjust stop-loss orders to lock in profits as the market moves in your favor. This dynamic approach can help maximize gains while protecting against reversals.

Best Stop Loss Strategies for Options

Different stop-loss strategies cater to varying trading styles and market conditions:

- Trailing Stop Loss: Automatically adjusts the stop level as the market moves in your favor, locking in profits.
- Volatility Stop: Sets stop levels based on the underlying asset's volatility, protecting against unexpected market swings.
- Profit Limit: Establishes a specific profit level at which to exit the trade, ensuring realized gains.
- Risk Reversal: Balances a position by owning a put and writing a call, providing downside protection with upside potential.
- Contrarian Stop: Targets a specific percentage above the current price, protecting against market sentiment shifts.
- Time Stop: Closes the position at a predetermined future time, regardless of the market condition, focusing on the time element in options trading.

Staying Informed and Educated

Continuous education is crucial in options trading. Stay updated with market trends, learn from experienced traders, and regularly engage in educational activities. Knowledge is a powerful tool in protecting your options and enhancing your trading skills.

As we conclude this chapter, remember that protecting your options is an ongoing process that involves careful planning, risk management, and emotional control. These principles lay the foundation for a successful and sustainable trading career. With this knowledge, you're equipped to navigate the options market with a balanced approach, ready for the advanced concepts and strategies that await in the subsequent chapters.

III

Controlling your Options

As we embark on the final chapter of our journey, we focus on solidifying the control over your options trading endeavors. This chapter encapsulates the transition from learning the basics to achieving mastery in options trading, highlighting key areas for sustained success and growth.

1. Continual Evaluation and Adaptation

In the dynamic world of options trading, constant evaluation and adaptation of your strategies are crucial. Embracing technologies like Artificial Intelligence can provide a significant edge. AI systems can analyze market patterns, news, and political events, offering insights for more informed decision-making. Additionally, options trading bots, with their advanced algorithms, can assist in real-time market analysis and strategy optimization.

1. Data-Driven Decision Making

Data is the backbone of successful trading. Utilize market data, historical trends, and global events to shape your strategies. Keep a meticulous record of your trades, as this historical data is invaluable in refining future strategies and understanding market dynamics.

1. Cultivating Discipline

Discipline is both a mental and physical exercise. Engage in activities like meditation or yoga to enhance mental clarity and focus. Set aside dedicated time for learning and practicing new strategies. Embrace the unpredictable nature of the markets, and be prepared to adapt your strategies in response to losses or market shifts.

1. Setting Realistic Goals

Options trading is a marathon, not a sprint. Set achievable goals, whether they be monthly or annual targets, and commit to them. Adjust your strategies as needed, but avoid the temptation to chase unrealistic returns or to move your stop-loss orders in pursuit of higher gains.

1. Personal Well-being

A healthy mind and body are essential for effective trading. Ensure you take breaks, engage in physical activities, and maintain a balanced diet. Remember, trading under stress or fatigue can lead to poor decision-making.

1. Learning from Mistakes

Every trader makes mistakes, but the key to growth is learning from them. Analyze your trading history to identify areas for improvement. Embrace mistakes as opportunities for learning, not as reasons for self-criticism.

1. Lifelong Learning

The financial markets are ever-evolving, so your education should be ongoing. Stay updated with the latest market trends, trading strategies, and global economic conditions. Continuous learning is essential to stay ahead in the dynamic world of options trading.

Last Option

In this final chapter, aptly titled "Last Option," you've delved into the depths of options trading, gaining valuable insights and knowledge along the way. As you now prepare to close the book on this comprehensive guide, it's crucial to understand that your journey in options trading is far from over. In fact, it's just beginning.

As you've advanced through the pages of "Last Option," you've honed your skills, deepened your understanding of market dynamics, and learned to read options chains effectively. You've also developed the ability to assess the probability of success for your trades, considering factors like buy/sell volume, open interest, and delta. This guide has equipped you with a robust foundation, covering everything from the fundamentals to advanced strategies, setting the stage for your journey ahead.

However, it's vital to recognize that the keys to success in options trading go beyond knowledge alone. While strategy and expertise are crucial, they are only part of the equation. Dedication, discipline, and the willingness to continuously learn and adapt are equally important. Options trading is a dynamic field, and to thrive in it, you must remain agile and open to change.

As you turn the final page of "Last Option" and venture into the world of options trading, remember that your path is unique, and your success is a reflection of your dedication and commitment. Embrace the challenges that lie ahead, celebrate your victories, and always approach the market with the curiosity and humility of a lifelong student.

With the right mindset and approach, the world of options trading offers endless possibilities for growth and success. So, as you embark on this journey, keep the spirit of "Last Option" alive in your trading endeavors. Your final option is the realization that, in the world of finance, learning never truly ends, and your potential for success is limitless.

Key Options Trading Terms and Explanations

In this section, we provide concise definitions and explanations of key terms used in options trading. This glossary is designed to help you familiarize yourself with the jargon and concepts you'll encounter in your trading journey.

Option: A financial derivative that gives the buyer the right, but not the obligation, to buy or sell an underlying asset at a specified price within a specified time frame.

Call Option: An option contract that gives the holder the right to buy the underlying asset at a specified price within a specified period.

Put Option: An option contract that gives the holder the right to sell the underlying asset at a specified price within a specified period.

Strike Price: The specified price at which the underlying asset can be bought or sold under an option contract.

Expiration Date: The date on which an option contract becomes void and the right to exercise it no longer exists.

Premium: The price paid by the buyer to the seller to acquire the rights granted by an option.

In the Money (ITM): Describes an option with intrinsic value. For call options, this is when the underlying asset's price is above the strike price. For put options, it's when the asset's price is below the strike price.

Out of the Money (OTM): Describes an option with no intrinsic value. For call options, this is when the underlying asset's price is below the strike price. For put options, it's when the asset's price is above the strike price.

At the Money (ATM): Describes an option where the underlying asset's price is equal to the strike price.

Delta: A measure of how much the price of an option is expected to move per one dollar change in the underlying asset.

Theta: A measure of the rate of decline of an option's value due to the passage of time, also known as time decay.

Gamma: A measure of the rate of change in delta over time as the underlying asset price changes.

Vega: A measure of an option's sensitivity to changes in the volatility of the underlying asset.

Rho: A measure of an option's sensitivity to changes in the interest rate.

Hedging: The practice of opening a position in the market to offset the risk of another position.

Stop Loss Order: An order placed with a broker to buy or sell once the stock reaches a certain price, used to limit a loss or protect a profit.

Leverage: The use of various financial instruments or borrowed capital to increase the potential return of an investment.

Volatility: A statistical measure of the dispersion of returns for a given security or market index, often used as a measure of risk.

Liquidity: The degree to which an asset can be quickly bought or sold in the market without affecting its price.

Open Interest: The total number of outstanding option contracts that have not been settled.

This glossary covers the basic terms you'll frequently encounter in options trading. Understanding these terms is crucial for effective communication and comprehension in the options market. As you progress in your trading journey, you'll likely encounter more specific terms, which you can add to your growing lexicon of trading knowledge.